PARABLES

PARABLES

TORIN M. FINSER, PhD

SteinerBooks | 2018

2018
SteinerBooks

An imprint of Anthroposophic Press, Inc.
610 Main Street, Great Barrington, MA 01230
www.steinerbooks.org

Thanks to Melissa Merkling for her editing.

Cover photo © by René LeBeau (Shutterstock)
Design: Jens Jensen

LIBRARY OF CONGRESS CONTROL NUMBER: 2018946438

ISBN 978-1-62148-230-7 (paperback)
ISBN 978-1-62148-231-4 (ebook)

CONTENTS

This book is dedicated to

Lise Jensen

and the beautiful island of Bornholm.

Beauty inspires creativity!

PREFACE

On the small Swedish island of Hven (7 ½ square kilometers, located between Scania and Zealand), in the town of Uraniborg one can find the home of the famous astronomer Tycho Brahe. Over the entrance to his home a few words are inscribed that express much of what is presented in this little book:

"By looking down I see up"

and

"By looking up I see down"

As I have worked with them, parables involve "looking down" (or out) to find an often overlooked object, and then "looking up" to the eternal truth that can be brought down to children.

How can we strive to do both? Can we teach our children to see not only what is on the desks before them, as well as what surrounds them in nature and in circles above them in the starry heavens? Parables may help us.

WHAT IS A PARABLE?

If one stops to ask, those that have a response often mention parables found in the Bible, such as this one from Mark:

> Hearken; Behold, there went out a sower to sow:
> And it came to pass, as he sowed, some fell by
> the way side, and the fowls of the air came and
> devoured it up. And some fell on stony ground,
> where it had not much earth; and immediately
> it sprang up, because it had no depth of earth:
> But when the Sun was up, it was scorched; and
> because it had no root, it withered away. And
> some fell among thorns, and the thorns grew
> up, and choked it, and it yielded no fruit. And
> other fell on good ground, and did yield fruit
> that sprang up and increased; and brought forth,
> some thirty, and some sixty, and some an hun-
> dred. And he said unto them, He that hath ears
> to hear, let him hear. (Mark 4:3–9, KJV)

Indeed, there are many more parables that are told in various sacred texts. What they have in common is often a simple narrative that speaks of larger truths, such as the one above. In the case of the seeds, one can easily see the relation to speaking and listening and the fertile ground of the soil (or the soul). Just as the ground needs to be fertile, so the listener needs to have the ears to hear.

However, one should not let historical or religious traditions detract from a fresh look at parables. As with so many things today, we need to find our own relationship to the creative process and put aside any inhibiting concepts from the past.

Many simple fables and short stories have parable qualities, such as these fables of Aesop:

"The Ant and the Grasshopper"
"The Boy Who Cried Wolf"
"The Fox and the Crow"
"The Lion and the Mouse"
"The Tortoise and the Hare"
"The Town Mouse and the Country Mouse"

Thus, for example, in "The Town Mouse and the Country Mouse," one realizes at the end once again the truth of "east, west, home is best." We each have our own sense of belonging and a place called home, whether in a big city or a cottage in the country. There is something reassuring about knowing where we belong, and thanks to two endearing mice, we are reminded of that fact through a simple fable.

Often a parable speaks to human foibles and temptations, urging us on to practice self-education, as seen in the Buddhist parable, "All is vanity":

> A rare species of monkey lived in the Himalayas. Hunters set up a trap to capture the monkeys, because they wished to collect their rare and prized blood. The monkeys were clever and skilled at avoiding traps but couldn't resist rice wine and fancy shoes, so the hunters set up a trap with rice wine barrels and dancing clogs. The monkeys saw that it was a trap but still couldn't resist drinking the wine and dancing in the shoes, and the hunters captured and killed them.

The parable illustrates how people often give in to temptation, even when they know it is bad for them, so the best thing to do is to find a way to give up all desire and seek reincarnation in an afterlife free of suffering and temptation.

In just a few lines, the story of the vain monkeys manages to communicate so much. One could say that a parable contains a larger lesson in a bite-sized portion. Using other words, a parable is a simple short story used to illustrate a moral or spiritual lesson. Dictionary.com describes a parable as "1. a short allegorical story designed to illustrate or teach some truth, religious principle, or moral lesson. 2. A statement or comment that conveys a meaning indirectly by the use of comparison, analogy, or the like."

The word *parable* can be traced back to Middle English and Old French origins as *parabole* and to the ecclesiastical Latin sense of *parabola*, meaning "discourse, allegory, or comparison."

To summarize, a parable

- discloses or reveals an eternal truth;
- helps us overcome temptations or illusions;
- educates from the simple "seed" to the larger reality, "wisdom."

Parables use comparison, allegory, imagery, analogy, or a short story to convey a larger meaning.

Many Waldorf teachers are familiar with the pedagogical story, a narrative often composed to meet the particular need in a child. These tend to be much longer than parables, and often have multiple images and characters. I find it more challenging to compose a concise parable that attempts to say as much as possible in a few words. The message also tends to be much more focused in a parable than in a pedagogical story, and parables do not usually comprise the main content of the lesson but are brought during "between" moments in the day. This gives them the aura of "off the cuff" telling, which can make it easier for some to assimilate. Spontaneity can leave the teacher (or parent) room for inspiration during the telling. Often the best endings arise when, surrounded by a group of children, one is able to ride their interest in the moment.

WHY PARABLES?

When I was a teacher of elementary-school children, I often found myself in unexpected situations. A lesson that I had carefully prepared would be finished a few minutes early, or the Spanish teacher might be late due to a longer transition with another class. Sometimes I needed something to help a group of children refocus or simply to fill the space for a few minutes with content so the class would remain quiet. Starting with practical necessity, I started telling an anecdote from home life, an event on a recent trip, or an amusing story from my life outside of school. After some time, I found that a parable often held their attention and allowed me to bring meaning rather than just a couple of minutes of "entertainment."

Then I began training myself to observe more carefully and draw the students' attention to commonplace objects around them. We need future scientists, and the best place to start is learning to observe! So I would pick up a pencil, a sheet of paper, or a stone someone had found outside and begin with a description that attempted to be as objective as possible:

> This pencil is yellow—a light yellow. There is some writing in silver that I can barely see (even at this stage, some are craning their necks to see), and the tip is very sharp. At the other end, I see a band of gold metal with a pink stub at the end (and even if some called out "That is the eraser!" I would continue with the description until finished).

But what really made the two-minute lesson interesting was the personal challenge I set for myself: is there a larger truth or meaning that I can draw from this object? Sometimes my ending was quite lame, and I was grateful when the Spanish teacher finally arrived and they could embark on more interesting journeys. Other times, however, I learned to seize the moment and conclude with a short summary that lifted the whole phenomenon into another realm. For the pencil, one such example had a touch of social inclusion: "Is it not interesting that this same object can write the most beautiful poem or a mean sentence about someone else?"

No need to say more. In fact, I found that less was more. Most of the "air time" in that two-minute parable was spent on the description, and the "message" at the end was always very brief. Otherwise it could easily become a preachy lesson in morality, which would probably have turned off my students more than helping any in need of social sensitivity.

Over time, parables became my friends. They helped me overcome unexpected situations and offered a seemingly casual context in which to communicate something the class needed to hear. As the years went by, I schooled myself in observing, finding and drawing forth parables in the most remarkable contexts. Life became more exciting and interesting, and the class would often know that they had better pay attention so as not to miss what would be the shortest lesson of the day.

Thanks to looping (the Waldorf journey of the class teacher over many years) I was able to tailor the parables to the needs of my students in age-appropriate ways. Some of the examples in this booklet will have such indications. But most exhilarating of all, at least for me, was the challenge of taking the same object, such as the pencil, and telling it differently in various contexts. It made a world of difference if that self-same pencil was being used to write an early composition or to make geometric drawings. We need to see the multiple purposes and facets in all aspects of life around us.

An environmental agenda also emerged as we went along. I found that, when someone had mistreated something from nature or when supplies were being consumed wantonly, a parable often helped raise consciousness. A sheet of paper bunched up and thrown away after a misspelled word could be retrieved, unfolded and redeemed through a parable. So rather than the "word of the day" that adorns many classrooms today, the notion of "respect" or "care" or "listening" could be fostered through the adept use of a parable rather than a moral admonition. For the beauty of a well-told parable is that each child seems to hear what is needed most by that individual. Sometimes the next day, or even weeks later, someone would whisper in my ear, "Mr. Finser, it is just like that parable you told about the seashell." They knew that I knew, and in such sharing we became a learning community.

OBJECTIVE AND SUBJECTIVE

As a consultant who works with schools in many countries, I have frequently found that people struggle with issues of trust. Beneath that initial finding there is often a long narrative of interpersonal struggle, sometimes based on strong personalities. Under that layer, one can find an undertone of subjectivity and opinion. Sometimes people frame an issue or see another person almost exclusively in terms of prior encounters and preconceived notions. When one traces those layers back to the core, it often comes down to a need to clear the "lenses" and see others with fresh eyes. I sometimes suggest that people walk into their next meeting with a beginner's mind and with the attitude, "I have never known this person in this context before. What can I experience today in a new way?"

In a lecture in Zürich on October 10, 1916, Rudolf Steiner described how people during the Greco–Roman time developed relationships very quickly. A person's mind worked more spiritually and could readily enter the thoughts of another person. Today many people can recognize a plant on first impression; similarly, people back then could do this in initial encounters. Today it takes much more time to get to know another person's thoughts and feelings. Why?

Starting with the printed word, new communications tools and modern transportation have allowed for much more contact, but often those contacts with others are less personal. It is easier to communicate but more difficult to build relationships, both to the natural world and to other human beings. Rudolf Steiner tells us:

> Humanity is being developed by the consciousness soul, making us much more separated and individual, leading more to egoism and to awareness of our isolation within our own body. Because of our consciousness soul, we are now more separate as individuals, as hermits who wander through the world. (Steiner, p. 73)

Without the innate tools to really find one another, we are more susceptible to bias and prejudice. Much that is said in communication is highly subjective. How can we work to overcome this tendency?

In our families and classrooms, we can try and discipline ourselves to speak precisely, based upon objective observations. So when I introduce the parable exercise in my Antioch University Waldorf teacher training class, I tell my students to pick an object and describe it in such a way that anyone else could pick up the same object and do the same. The pencil is either yellow or red. It has an eraser or it does not. Objectivity is built on the hard facts of accurate observation. We all need to train ourselves to state what we see, and not always immediately go to what we feel or think.

Parenthetically, when I do administrative and leadership training, I often set up observation groups to look for things such as body language, "air time," speaking patterns, and the like. When the groups give feedback, I encourage them to begin their sentences with the words "I observed.... I saw.... I heard...." Such observations should be so transparent that anyone could have delivered them. This gives us all a common ground for agreement. Objectivity is like the foundation upon which the social house can be built.

Then, in parable formation, there is the opposite element. Once the object has been described in a manner so objective anyone else could have done it, I ask participants to try to find a subjective interpretation, a hidden meaning that can be lifted out of the experience. In this realm, each person in the room might have a different response. And that is okay. We have given the subjective a place to live and, by doing so, have brought consciousness to the stark difference between objectivity and subjectivity.

The ultimate test of this last step is to have someone describe the pencil (in the same way that anyone else would have done), and then ask each person in the room to find a different conclusion to the parable of the pencil. The multiplicity of interpretation is then welcomed.

We need to reach a place in our school communities where the hard facts can be viewed with as much objectivity as possible; then the ground is solid and upon which multiple perspectives can build the structure of understanding. In the end, the goal is to find insight that leads to informed decisions. We need social technique to build community.

PARABLES AND NATURE

In his seminal book, *Last Child in the Woods: Saving Our Children from Nature-Deficit Disorder*, Richard Louv talks about the growing issue of nature-deficit disorder:

> Within the space of few decades, the way children understand and experience nature has changed radically. The polarity of the relationship has reversed. Today's kids are aware of the global threats to the environment—but their physical contact, their intimacy with nature, is fading. That's exactly the opposite of how it was when I was a child.... Our society is teaching young people to avoid direct experience in nature. That lesson is delivered in schools, families, even organizations devoted to the outdoors, and codified into the legal and regulatory structures of many of our communities....
>
> Yet, at the very moment that the bond is breaking between the young and the natural world, a growing body of research links our mental, physical and spiritual health directly to our associations with nature—in positive ways.

Several of these studies suggest that thoughtful exposure of youngsters to nature can even be a powerful form of therapy for attention-deficit disorders and other maladies. As one scientist puts it, we can now assume that just as children need good nutrition and adequate sleep, they may very well need contact with nature.

Reducing that deficit—healing the broken bond between our young and nature—is in our self-interest, not only because aesthetics or justice demands it, but also because our mental, physical, and spiritual health depends upon it. (Louv, pp. 1–3)

Parables offer an opportunity to help children reconnect with nature. Even in an urban environment, parents and teachers can find many parables from the natural world. A walk in the park, the clouds in the sky, falling rain or a cactus on a windowsill...the possibilities are endless. At a time when so many children live in virtual worlds, we have a serious obligation to help them reconnect with nature-based learning.

It is not just about "love of the outdoors" and all things natural. This urgent plea, as Richard Louv so eloquently states, is all about mental, physical, and spiritual health. Sensory education is essential for our development as human beings, and how we are as human beings has a great deal to do with our social interactions and the state of world affairs.

In my recent book *Education for Nonviolence*, I devoted an entire chapter to the importance of sensory education. For the purposes of this work with parables, I would like to highlight just one aspect of the senses—the inherent wisdom bestowed on us through our many senses. In a lecture on February 22, 1916, Rudolf Steiner describes how our sense organs, which we mostly carry externally (eyes, ears, nose) are the product of many, many years of evolution. They serve us as they do now thanks to a long spiritual process. Our skin, for example—something we generally take for granted—is actually a highly developed sense organ. When we touch, see, hear, and so on, we are using highly refined instruments.

Many of the conveniences of our modern world have had unintended consequences in regard to the senses. We appreciate air conditioning, downloading information from the internet, and communicating efficiently through email, yet all things come with a price. Optometrists report an increase in macular degeneration. Conditions that used to affect people in old age, especially those who spent much time outdoors without sunglasses, are now showing up in teenagers who spend hours exposed to the blue light of an iPad and other electronic screens. Likewise, teachers have reported a general lessening in the capacity to hear, let alone differentiate sounds. In numbing our senses we risk personal health and increase the chances of social isolation.

Parables are a call to notice, to listen, to see, to observe. Teachers and parents might not feel they are particularly skilled in telling parables, but the very attempt to reconnect with objects around us, natural and otherwise, brings many benefits. Just as we all need exercise to remain fit, children also need to experience things firsthand to remain whole. Technology is a tool, but when it becomes a preoccupation, it can sever us from the natural world. We need to lift our eyes from the keyboard (at least every 20 minutes, we are told) and see the world around us!

SOME EXAMPLES

A Broken Branch

As I walked by our holly bush, I saw some dead brown leaves, which led my gaze to a small branch hanging to one side in defeat. As I plucked it off, the leaves were crisp, dry, and utterly dead. I wondered if the branch had been injured by the house painter and his ladder or perhaps by a slab of ice falling from the roof in the spring thaw? I clipped it off and then I went on with life.

Many months later, while passing that same bush, I noticed something different: red berries against the dark green of the holly. Their bright colors made me very happy.

When we experience a setback or just a bad day, it helps to remember the berries that grow even on a wounded bush.

A Blackberry—For a Younger Child

"Look Mom, I just found this great big blackberry! I have never seen one so large. Do you want to eat it with me?"

"Yes, of course. Look at all the small parts that make it so big...how many bumps do you think are on this one? It is just like our big family."

A Blackberry—For Someone Slightly Older

"Can I eat this one?"

"No, it is not ripe yet."

"Why?"

"It still needs more days in the sunshine."

"But now that I picked it, will the Sun still warm it and make it yummy?"

"No, that one will never become good to eat. It was picked before it was ready."

Note: That may be enough. But when the next round of questions come, such as "Why is my older sister allowed to watch that movie and I am not?" it might be possible to say, "It is not the right time; you are not old enough. Everything has a right time."

A Blackberry—Perhaps for Early Adolescence

Ouch, that hurt. I had no idea that berry bush had such sharp prickles (not thorns). Look at this one, it is stuck in my finger...greenish-brown, curved, and sharp as a hook.

Sometimes the most appealing things, such as blackberries, come at a price. Watch out what you wish for!

Or, some days later, a simple one-liner follow-up: Have you ever wondered why the biggest, juiciest blackberries are often the hardest to reach?

The Rosehip

Round and red as a cherry tomato, the rosehip in my hand is ever so smooth. Yet the greenish-brown stem has prickles and is quite twisted. It was so appealing I had to pick it from the bush. Yet when I started to open it I was warned, "Be careful and wear gloves; you will become itchy using your bare hands!"

Oh well, I guess some things are better left alone.

A Feather

I found this feather on the side of a pathway near the beach. As you can see it is very small, but ever so soft when you stroke it across your hand. It is mostly white, but near the tip it turns a light grey. The stem runs right up the middle, but it, too, is very flexible. Near the base are tufts that seem more like fur. Oops, it just blew out of my hand, it is so light...it must love to play with the wind.

The seagull that shed this feather must have been flying over this place recently. If only I could be so light of heart I, too, might be able to soar upward into the heavens.

DEER

The other day I saw a mother deer with two newborn fawns. She was grazing on the low-hanging leaves of an apple tree. Her fur was soft brown; her eyes were round and dark; and she did not move as she looked at me for a long time. (Her little ones scampered into the underbrush.) But what struck me most were her large ears, brown on the outside and white inside and cupped and pointed in my direction. I felt she was observing me with her ears as well as her eyes.

Maybe we should all learn to listen like a deer.

Sunglasses—For a Somewhat Older Child

I found my sunglasses. They were under the seat of my car...! These are the ones I bought on vacation, with the thin, silver frame. They are so light I barely feel them when they are on my nose. The lenses really protect my eyes, but they make everything seem a bit darker.

There are, of course, many different types of glasses, and as you know the lenses can be adjusted for reading or for looking into the distance while driving. But even without glasses, we each have our own lenses inside our eyes. We each see things differently; just as we each have our own lenses, we need to remember that there are many ways to see things.

Heather on the Rocky Shore

Walking along the shore in Bornholm, Denmark, we saw a large, ancient boulder perched on the left bank. It had a crack running diagonally from right to left, and much to my surprise I found a tiny bush growing in that very small space. It had small, pointed green leaves and purple blossoms. Some of the tips of the blossoms were tinged with white, and they smelled of sea air.

How could something so delicate grow in the mere crack of a boulder along a windswept shore? Sometimes hardship and struggle produce inner strength and beauty.

FORMING A PARABLE

There are, no doubt, many ways to prepare a parable, and the best ones are usually those that are truly discovered. However, here are a few suggestions from many years as a collector of parables.

Most parents and teachers carry questions, interest, uncertainty, and sometimes concerns about a child. Often it is simply a child's need to be seen and affirmed, or it may involve a social issue. Some children learn more slowly than others, or there might be a life event in the family such as the birth of a sibling or the illness of a beloved grandparent. A teacher's concern can awake interest that can become care and even love. We open our mind and heart to whatever is going on in that young person's life.

Out of this general caring, I have often found that things can crystallize into one main issue, such as recognition, teasing, loss, need for more joy, and so on. It helps if one can sort things out a bit and decide to work on one aspect for a while and carry it in one's child-rearing backpack, so to speak.

Then, with this one aspect in the backpack, I start to travel with eyes and ears wide open. Walking is one of my favorite activities. It is amazing the things we can find on a long walk! One has to be truly open to sense impressions and to nature. If one goes out with the idea of finding something, one is quite limited. It is best to simply walk with the question(s) in the backpack, for if one is open to encountering objects, sights, and sounds in nature, there is often a moment of magic—there, right before our eyes is something that speaks to the issue buried in the heart (or backpack). A stone jumps out of the path, a feather falls to the ground, or one turns a corner to behold an amazing sunset. Out of the welter of sense impressions, something jumps out to say, "Here I am. Use me to help with your parable!"

Sometimes one reaches a dead end, which is natural. At least one has gotten some good exercise. At times, I will have spent days looking for the parable that can help a particular child, only to find one that will help someone else instead; that is okay. When we work too hard at something, the solution often eludes us. The key is being open to the sense impressions and letting them speak to us.

Yet if one finds an object (I recommend using concrete objects, at least in the early years), then the next level of work begins. Each thing has its own language; it is important to let the object speak. In the preceding examples, I had three rounds with blackberries, each time finding new aspects (and of course, eating a few along the way). What is the blackberry telling me? What can I see, smell, and feel? It is important to live into the experience without abstract conceptualization.

Over time, something else starts to emerge. The previously described feather sat on my shelf for twenty-four hours before I was ready to formulate the parable, for the next stage is most delicate: What does this object say that speaks to a higher reality? What is the divine essence contained in this little thing? A feather is a very different reality from a blackberry. The whole gesture, quality, and experience of being a blackberry is completely different from being a feather.

To form a parable one has to "be the thing" and live into it as completely as possible. This makes it possible for another kind of magic to appear—the leap into a message that can speak to a particular child or group. The phenomenon, when fully experienced, can give birth to a message, a pearl of wisdom that speaks eternally.

Then I try to write it all down.

Finally, I edit as much as possible—with few exceptions, the shorter the parable the better it will be. ("A Park Bench," which follows, will be one.) But especially with the final message in a parable, one needs brevity to avoid pedantry. To summarize, here are some of the steps in birthing a parable:

1. Let your love, general interest, and concern crystallize into a question regarding a particular child. Put it in your backpack.
2. Take a walk with the senses wide open to new experiences.
3. Let something jump out at you; stop and observe.
4. Let the object or experience speak.
5. Draw out the wisdom that could help the child you have been thinking about.
6. Write and edit.

Then comes the glorious moment when one can take that parable into the classroom or the home to share. One has to find the right moment. It cannot be forced into a lesson or over dinner. Some parables are meant to be shared with a group, others one-on-one. One needs a certain amount of intuition for finding *kairos*, the right time and place.

Most often, our interest in the object in question acts like a magnet; it draws others to it. We must be sincere of course, and the joy of discovery will be infectious. By the way, our enthusiasm also educates. I remember one of my teachers, Lee Lecraw, presenting plants in a botany class at the Waldorf Institute in Garden City. She was so enthralled with each specimen, found so many ways to draw us into the experience, that we all wanted to become botanists! To have such enthusiasm, *en-theos*, is to be close to God.

Within a short parable that might take only a couple of minutes to tell we have many of the key elements of Waldorf education: phenomenology that builds a foundation for scientific inquiry, the oral culture of telling and sharing, a holistic attitude toward nature and the human being, and the joy of teaching from direct experience. A teacher or parent who can bring this to a child has really done a deed for humanity.

IN PRAISE OF SCIENCE

Much has been made of the importance of teaching science to children and, later, to students in high school. Yet, what so often passes for science is really a collection of theories with a few examples or "experiments." Waldorf schools build the capacity for science from the ground up, so to speak, by focusing on phenomenology and the ability to observe. In age-appropriate ways, teachers introduce their students to botany, physics, chemistry, and much more, always beginning with what can be experienced before coaching them toward a gradual awakening of thought.

In the context of this short piece on parables, I would like to observe that a teacher needs to be sure all statements made in class are accurate, and when something is controversial or might not be part of the commonly understood basis of scientific thought, teachers need to contextualize their statements with phrases such as "some people say..." or "Waldorf teachers I spoke with have told me..." In parent evenings, teachers are well advised to alert parents *ahead of time* to any concepts based on an anthroposophic view of science and might be challenged by conventional scientists. Waldorf teachers have every right to teach science using Waldorf methods, but just assuming that parents will always go along with the flow could be a grave error.

Likewise, even if one is developing a parable on blackberries, for example, it helps if the teacher spends a few minutes researching and downloading facts on the subject. We need both feet on the ground—knowing what is commonly available *and* understanding Waldorf methods. These two "legs" are mutually supportive and help us connect with parents and potential parents in the community.

Moreover, it is fun to learn more, even while enjoying a bowl of blackberries and milk. In a recent search online, Wikipedia gave me the following:

> Blackberries are perennial plants that typically bear biennial stems ("canes") from the perennial root system. During its first year, a new stem (the primocane) grows vigorously to its full length of three to six meters (up to nine meters in some cases), arching or trailing along the ground and bearing large palmately

compound leaves with five or seven leaflets. It does not produce any flowers. In its second year, the cane becomes a floricane, and the stem does not grow longer, but the lateral buds break to produce flowering laterals (which have smaller leaves with three or five leaflets).

First- and second-year shoots usually have numerous short-curved, very sharp prickles that are often erroneously called thorns.... Unmanaged mature plants form a tangle of dense arching stems, the branches rooting from the node tip on many species when they reach the ground. Vigorous and growing rapidly in woods, scrub, hillsides, and hedgerows, blackberry shrubs tolerate poor soils, readily colonizing wasteland, ditches, and vacant lots.

Blackberry leaves are food for certain caterpillars. Some grazing mammals, especially deer, are also very fond of the leaves. Caterpillars of the concealer moth *Alabonia geoffrella* have been found feeding inside dead blackberry shoots. When mature, the berries are eaten and their seeds dispersed by several mammals, such as the red fox and the Eurasian badger, as well as by small birds. (YouTube, "Wild Blackberries")

Often when one researches facts on a subject, it leads to other possible strands of teaching—in this case, the relationship to geography, which, parenthetically, is currently a dying subject in many schools:

> Blackberries grow wild throughout most of Europe and are an important element of the ecology in many countries, where harvesting the berries is a popular pastime. However, the plants are also considered a weed, sending roots down from branches that touch the ground, and sending up suckers from the roots. In some parts of the world without native blackberries, such as in Australia, Chile, New Zealand, and the Pacific Northwest of North America, some blackberry species, particularly *Rubus armeniacus* (Himalayan blackberry) and *Rubus laciniatus* (evergreen blackberry), are naturalized and considered an invasive species and a serious weed. ("Blackberry," Wikipedia)

Observing, looking things up, deciding which facts are significant, and then observing again may seem like a lot of work for a short parable, but it helps us prepare for unanticipated questions that may come our way, even days later.

ANOTHER WAY

My students in Waldorf teacher education courses at Antioch University know that I often say, "Now that we've covered that aspect, let's look at it from another perspective." Just when they think, "I've got it," we turn the tables and start anew. This method is deliberate, as good teachers need to see each lesson, and indeed each student, from many angles. There is nothing worse than labeling or holding onto fixed notions about individual children, which holds them in that straitjacket so that they cannot grow. As Goethe once said, we need to treat people not as they are but as they hope to become. Looking at things from multiple perspectives is a good practice for our social future.

Therefore, having just laid out a step-by-step approach to forming a parable in the previous section, I will share another pathway—that of the narrative. It still has an object and a message, but the approach is that of the gently meandering brook in contrast to droplets of water falling off a rock. Of the two, I still prefer the former, as it carries with it a huge effort in self-discipline to work purely from the object–phenomena and not to go into the storytelling mode, which many teachers prefer. Nevertheless, the following example is different, and the reader may appreciate some value in drawing forth a parable as a "musing" narrative intended for adults.

A PARK BENCH

Walking with my family in the park below Edinburgh Castle in early August 2015, we found children playing, families with strollers, couples in conversation, a variety of concession stands, winding pathways, and ever so many park benches. They were essentially all alike, about six feet in length, less than half that in height, with grey timber slats and concrete supporting legs. Most of the benches had plaques in the middle of the backrest that remember someone who had passed on. They were sturdy, simple, and showed every sign of weathering the ravages of Scottish weather. An ordinary sight by most accounts, and something many would pass by without a thought, unless they are tired and in need of a rest.

Then I began to look more closely. One bench held a homeless man who was slumped over, wrapped in many clothes, and assiduously avoiding eye contact with passersby. Another featured a young woman, an office worker perhaps, enjoying her last sips of a latte before heading back to work. One bench held a father and two sons, perhaps eight and ten, each with an ice cream cone. Yet another bench had a young family with two strollers and one slightly older, more mobile boy darting in and out of the pedestrian traffic and causing slight fits of anxiety for his parents. Still one more bench featured two lovers lost in an embrace.

These benches all told stories of which I had but a fleeting glimpse. I could not really know the lives of those involved, whether they were happy or sad, healthy or sick, successful or not. As with so many things in life, there was clearly more I did not know than what I could perceive in passing—yet it got me thinking.

A bench is really a wonderful invention: open to all, unconditionally hospitable, yet unassuming. Aside from an occasional lick of paint, a park bench asks little for itself, yet offers support and comfort to many. It is an open invitation.

People sit on benches for varying amounts of time, from the office worker with her latte cherishing a fifteen-minute break to the homeless man who may spend a good part of the day in that warm spot in the sun. The park bench does not discriminate, nor does it charge rent. Its services are freely offered, supporting passersby for a while before they move on.

The jobs we have in life are not really who we are. Our work is a place of focus, a place to return to again and again for a while before moving on. A good job will support us to an extent, but the job will always remain separate from our inner core, our essential self. No matter how much time we spend on any park bench, it will never become us. We alight for a while and then move on. Some may move from one bench to another, others may spend most of a career on one bench. But there will always be a distinction between my bench and me.

Let us not totally define ourselves by our jobs. Let us remember to listen to the inner stirring, the hopes and dreams nestled close to the heart. The wooden slats of a bench are there to provide support and help us do what we need to do, but there is no glue that holds us there forever. We are always free. Our choices are as abundant as we want them to be. We can rest and then move on again, not because of what others say, but by listening to our calling, our inner voice. Our destiny is greater than any park bench.

THE UNKNOWN

Having described the importance of sensory education through parables, I will briefly consider what cannot be understood fully just through the senses—what can, and perhaps should, always remain mysterious.

Owing to materialism, most people see "things" as all-important. This is clear when talk about those who drive fancy cars or have multiple houses or extensive wardrobes. Yet also those who struggle to put food on the table are often (by necessity in this case) focused on "things." In such cases it might be coupons for a supermarket, clothing on sale, or items purchased at a Dollar Store. We ignore at our peril the huge influence of economic disparity in our country when it comes to the "things," including those who have real needs to those who have ever-greater wants. All this is fed by the media and advertising, which constantly hold before our consciousness the possibility of new cravings and additional items to purchase. Advertising has created untold damage in terms of how we measure success according to material accumulation.

Waldorf communities are not immune to the ravages of materialism. Parents need to question themselves when replacing plastic with an abundance of wooden toys or replacing free public education with the "purchase" of a Waldorf education. Of course, food bought at the local farmers' market is healthier, and local co-ops are a wonderful place to shop. But have we simply replaced one expression of materialism with another? My children were all raised with wooden toys, healthy food (mostly), and a Waldorf education, so there should be no misunderstanding as to where I stand on these matters. However, I do suggest considering *how* we make these decisions and our deeply held motivations. Perhaps wanting "the best" for our children can be a subtler expression of consumerism?

A Waldorf education cannot be "purchased." Having put five children through Waldorf K–12, with one soon to graduate, I have come to view what they received as free gifts from their teachers. Tuition payments and salaries paid seem now to have had very little to do with what was gifted by the faculty. The payments made were simply steps toward supporting the career decisions of the teachers and a fraction of the total cost of running a school. When our children talk about their former teachers, it is clear that the value of the relationships and lessons taught had almost nothing to do with a common economic transaction. My children's teachers were able to see the potential in their students and educate them toward what they could become in future years. As with planting an orchard, it takes many years to harvest the results fully. We need to start looking at education in a similar fashion.

As described in previous pages, parables can train observation and honor the natural world around us, but they also lift our consciousness to the eternal found in all things. Thus we could say that a parable is a tiny step that can help us counter materialism.

I would like to go one step further. There are parables that are also riddles. As such, these can cultivate a sense for the mysterious and unknown. Rather than merely searching for answers through Google, some knowledge need time to mature. Not all questions can be satisfied with short, factual answers. Some things need time. The following are a few examples.

1) Standing in a field on the island of Bornholm, I can look out at the Baltic Sea stretching as far as the eye can see. The waves ripple in shades of ultramarine, emerald, and Prussian blue,

always alive and moving. Yet, as I stand on the grass, I notice that the water meets the horizon far above me. The horizon is higher than I am! How can the water be above me and yet not flood the land?

2) Holding a newborn grandchild recently, I wondered at the miracle before me. The perfectly formed hands and fingers, the rounded head and tiny nose. Where did this one come from? Glancing up at the parents, I felt immense gratitude that they had been gifted with such a child. And despite knowing both Mom and Dad quite well, I wondered how this little one would grow up to be a person, an individual, and someone who is not just a replica of parental genes. Where did this miracle come from?

3) When I sat with my mother during her last hours on this Earth, she said a few words intended to help us deal with her departure. Always full of love, she was thinking of her family, asking us to look at family photo albums and talking about vacations and memories that held us together. She was ready for her departure, and was simply trying to help us with that transition. Our hearts were open and vulnerable, and in that moment her spirit was strong.

How is it that death can be such a victory for the human spirit that longs to be once again free of a physical body?

Many more examples can be found of parables that speak to realities beyond usual comprehension. In each of the preceding examples, no one pulled out an iPhone for an "answer"; no one was being materialistic.

In our quest for reclaiming this Earth as a friendly host for the spirit, we have some very powerful allies. The three instances cited indicate some of them:

As mentioned, nature is our friend, a splendid example of transformation and metamorphosis that overcomes and endures. We all need to be good stewards of this God-given treasure all around us.

Birth and death are the great gateways to the spiritual world, and each time someone crosses the threshold on the inbound or outbound journey, there is an infusion of spirit into matter. Schools do well to build community and resilience around experiences of birth and death, as many Waldorf schools have done in the face of loss.

All those in the so-called helping professions—nurses, counselors, childcare services, community volunteers—are often those who have opened their hearts (and minds) to transformative processes. In our local communities, we often find some of those same people on the library fundraising committee, who also volunteer at the community kitchen and turn out for the arts festivals. Waldorf schools would do well to network and join with such wonderful people.

When working out at the Y or buying groceries at the co-op, I often find opportunities for good conversations and new perspectives on community life. As a teacher, I find these conversations are sometimes a treasure trove for discovering new ideas, awaking to resources near at hand for lessons, and even noticing new parables. The same faculties that serve us well in discovering parables also help in fostering community life, and vice versa. Whenever we lift our eyes to see people and things around us, we are also building community. Relationship is about both the seen and the unseen in life.

PARABLES AND TIME

Like a good bottle of wine, some parables age well with time. For a teacher it is a particularly good challenge to take a parable and allow metamorphosis through the elementary school grades. A pencil, blackberry, or feather can be brought back, each time in a different way.

One especially exciting element occurs when we take a central image and weave a tapestry of parables over time. For example, I will use the image of the sword. Some parents initially object to stories that have "warlike" images, but in my experience the Waldorf curriculum actually helps children transform such images far better than do the video games so many play after school. The following are a few instances of the sword in various grades:

> FIRST — The fairy tale of Briar Rose features many princes who try to cut their way through the thickets, only to have the story end with a kiss that dissolves an enchantment.

FOURTH — Balmung, the sword of Siegfried
in the Nibelungenlied, and Legbiter, the
sword of the Viking King Magnus Barelegs

FIFTH — The sword of Perseus, used to cut off
the head of Medusa

SIXTH — Durandal, the sword from the Song
of Roland and the history of Charlemagne

SIXTH OR SEVENTH — Excalibur, the sword
of King Arthur, given to him by the wise
Merlin

How can we weave parables from these sword images? One possibility is that, after the first day the lesson is presented, and after the second day, when the children participate in the retelling, and at the end of the third day, during which some aspects of the narrative find their way into projects, compositions, and writing in books, the teacher might wrap up the narrative with a short summary that lifts the central images to a new level of understanding. To illustrate, consider just one of the examples: Excalibur.

We have heard of King Arthur and how he had a mighty sword, Excalibur, given to him to help rule his people with strength, clarity, and compassion. It was his to use and then return. Where it is now? No one knows for sure.

As we consider Excalibur and the other swords we have heard about in past years, we need to use our thinking to compare and understand. Like a sword, human thought can be strong and clear. It is up to the hand that wields the sword and the person who thinks the thoughts whether they harm or serve others.

PARABLES THROUGH
THE SEASONS

One of the original teachers at Green Meadow Waldorf School told me that it was very important to teach an intensive block of mathematics before Michaelmas each school year. He went on to talk about the will and the importance of bringing thinking down into practice. I cannot recall if I managed to follow his advice in all instances, but it awakened in me the importance of how we place our subjects in relation to the seasons.

Certainly, some subjects lend themselves to certain seasons for obvious reasons, such as botany in the fall or spring or local geography or mineralogy when the outdoors is more available to those of us teaching in northern climes. Yet, in the spirit of the "exception to the rule" already discussed in the section "Another Way," I recently accompanied a fourth grade in Anchorage, trudging through the snow and intent on discovering all sorts of natural wonders. No matter what choices are made, I urge teachers to become a kind of "calendar of the soul," in which inner and outer life are held in companionship.

In regard to parables, one way to practice mindfulness of the changing seasons is to "adopt" a deciduous tree near the school. Imagine taking a class out there (again a northern perspective) after returning to school from the summer and relating a parable under the canopy of green leaves, only to return to the same tree during its fall foliage, then to the stark, barren exposure of winter, and finally during the onset of new buds in spring. Each time we might draw their attention to the tree and encourage more careful observation. Then the teacher could close the parable of the tree with a different aspect for each season:

> *Late summer.* Observations; then: We are lucky there are so many leaves above us to give us shade. If this tree had only one leaf, we would be very hot right now, but there are so many moving and fluttering above us that together they give us much-needed shade. So now, at the start of this new school year, we are once again a class, and because there are so many of us, we

will be able to do many things that any one of us could not do alone.

Fall. Observations; then: We are lucky this is a maple tree! We have learned so much about the different types of trees near our school. But because this is a maple, we have wonderfully bright reds, oranges, yellows, and just a bit of green left to see above us. There are already some brown leaves under our feet. On some days, someone in the class might be feeling like that bright yellow leaf, or the red one there, or even the brown one near my toes. All these leaves belong to the tree, and all our feelings are part of being a class.

Winter. Observations; then: Don't worry, we will not be out here very long. It is so cold. But here we are with our friend, the maple tree. It, too, seems cold, with scarcely a leaf left to be found on this snowy day. Yet here it still stands, tall and resolute. But deep inside, our tree is very much alive, thanks to the sap and the many layers of life under the bark. So there are times when we have to be strong and resolute when things are difficult. Inside each of us is our source of life, the courage that comes from the heart.

Spring. Observations; then: I know you have been waiting all morning to go outside on this beautiful spring day. Some of you have already told me about the buds on our maple tree. They are all over! This tree did make it through the winter, as we did as a class. Remember, just like the buds on our tree, there is always hope.

A good teacher will find many ways to travel through the year with an adopted tree, nearby stream, woodland glade or view of the clouds in the sky. No matter what the material, the children can be guided to reconnect with nature, appreciate seasonal changes, and learn to relate the wisdom of the natural world to the wisdom within each human being.

PARABLES AND
SELF-DEVELOPMENT
OF THE TEACHER

In the fall of 2017 I taught a workshop in Denver. We had just worked on the basic exercises Rudolf Steiner gave for self-development, and then a few students presented parables they had prepared overnight. Suddenly, I had a new insight; when done well, parables are not only good for our children, but can also aid in the development of a parent or teacher. Briefly, this is what came to me in that moment:

1. A parable is an invitation to focus on one object, to concentrating fully on what one is seeing without any distractions (*control of thought*).

2. To practice and prepare one's telling of a parable means one has to return to it again and again (as with the blackberries) and bring order to the will (*control of action*).

3. Along the way, there can be many disappointments and failed attempts, as well as

the joy of success as seen in the responses of children (*equanimity*).

4. Everything on this Earth has meaning and a lesson to reveal that can help us grow and develop (*positivity*).

5. To learn the deeper mysteries embedded in simple objects, one has to open the mind fully and see again and again with fresh eyes (*open-mindedness*).

Working with parables also schools the teacher.

CONCLUSION

To see a World in a Grain of Sand
And Heaven in a Wild Flower
Hold Infinity in the palm of your hand
And Eternity in an hour...
(WILLIAM BLAKE, *Auguries of Innocence*)

Finding a parable is to hold infinity in your hand. The smallest pebble or blade of grass can speak universal wisdom if we only have the eyes to see.

Seeing, however, is not simple these days. Whether in politics or the media, "alternative facts" arise and meet us everywhere. There are some who seriously question whether any story is true or if anyone can be trusted. We no longer have confidence in what we read, since so much is communicated virtually. In a world where there is so little trust, confidence, or believability we are susceptible to those who hold the reins to power and the all-important tools of communication. In coffee shops and at work, many today spend much their time complaining about our collective misery.

Thus it is more important than ever before that we look up, as well as down, seeing both the wildflowers and the stars at night. Children long for the joy that comes with discovery, the feel of rough granite or a smooth acorn, the smell of a field full of freshly cut hay or the sounds of a babbling brook. However, we can no longer just take children out into the world and expect this will happen on its own. Many have grown short-sighted and somewhat deaf to the wonders of nature. We need to lead our children back into nature and help them experience the sweet delights of sensory experience, for they long for peace, wholeness, and wonder.

Are we destined for only misery and despair, or can we "birth" something new?

> *Every Night and every Morn*
> *Some to Misery are Born*
> *Every Morn and every Night*
> *Some are Born to sweet delight.*
> *Some are Born to sweet delight*
> *Some are Born to Endless Night.*
> (ibid.)

There are many who long for a renaissance of soul and an awakening of the human spirit. As parents and teachers, we hold the future "in the palm of our hand."

BIBLIOGRAPHY

Louv, Richard, *Last Child in the Woods: Saving Our Children from Nature-Deficit Disorder*, Chapel Hill NC: Algonquin, 2008.

Steiner, Rudolf, *The Connection between the Living and the Dead*, Great Barrington MA: SteinerBooks, 2017.

OTHER BOOKS
BY TORIN FINSER

Education for Nonviolence: The Waldorf Way (2017)

Finding Your Self: Exercises and Suggestions to Support the Inner Life of the Teacher (2013)

Guided Self-Study: Rudolf Steiner's Path of Spiritual Development: A Spiritual-Scientific Workbook (2015)

In Search of Ethical Leadership: If not now, when? (2003)

Initiative: A Rosicrucian Path of Leadership (2011)

Leadership Development: Change from the Inside Out (2016)

Organizational Integrity: How to Apply the Wisdom of the Body to Develop Healthy Organizations (2007)

School as a Journey: The Eight-Year Odyssey of a Waldorf Teacher and His Class (1995)

School Renewal: A Spiritual Journey for Change (1999)

A Second Classroom: Parent-Teacher Relationships in a Waldorf School (2015)

Silence Is Complicity: A Call to Let Teachers Improve Our Schools through Action Research—Not NCLB (2007)

www.ingramcontent.com/pod-product-compliance
Lightning Source LLC
Chambersburg PA
CBHW032214040426
42449CB00005B/595